murmurs

a short collection of poems
written by Jessica O'Brien

First Printing: 2017

ISBN 978-0-692-89187-2

Jessica O'Brien
Redondo Beach, CA 90277

contents

one

one is red
a fast paced dance
it's a vast expanse- a wondrous wound
for the feeling of first to which i'm immune
one for the single last letter you sent me
one for the one time I tried to end me
one for the brave and the bleeding organ convulsing
gravely pleading with me it's still pulsing
one red prayer for the fleshy affair
for the corporal cage which houses awareness
one for the being the seeing the only
one for the it
and the best
and the lonely.

Mouth Poem

Porcelain boulders grace my shoulders
It's dark and deep and wet my
Head pulled forward, haunting horror
Breath on my back and my neck let
Shallow huffs disrupt my stance and a rough tongue scuff my knees as
she swallows and pants and forces a dance
A waltz of mute language,
fast-paced passive trance
Halitosis and anguish,
neurosis and rants
Blessed banter be a treat-
til words are all there's left to eat
and sweets in excess... arrest.
What words are spoken I don't understand:
Elusive excuses go down quite like sand
I grind grains with my molars, swallowing still
It's been years of chewing
yet I can't get my fill
I'll hide in the places where tastes never travel and
hold my tongue tightly for fear it unravels,
linger in whiles where I've vision *and* sight
and fight to remind my blood-gummed smile
that an unclenched jaw,
Raw riled and right,
despite what it swallows or sews
Saw more light.

EMPOWERMENT OF SPEECH

I want letters to permeate the air which surrounds me this
Extra two inches surrounding my body it
Changes with each movement but
I claim it
My Personal space,

And I know you don't like to be touched without warning but
I want my words to encapsulate your body
To prod at your person
Maybe even
correct your posture

I want my words to
Be ridiculously appropriate to
etch an unshakable sketch–
Please stir.

I want to fly your mind like a kite on a windy day
Make you think
Should I really be out here tugging on a string so that I can watch these
distant colors

And the answer is yes,
Because kites are magical
and in the off chance the wind is able to carry you away
All the better.

I want to hologramize my sentences
For a multidimensional image to actualize
With my
psychedelic diction
I want my words to
Diffuse resonance
Fill a room with wavy air for evidence

I'd like my language to be precise
from six lightyears away
An alien congregation cupping their hands to catch my
Fractalized drops of self referentiality

I will never cease these linguistic gymnastics
This shit is a playground.

Listen:
I want to make a deaf man wonder why these vibrations are so clear
He can read it on my lips,
But instead holds out his palm to feels the drips
of a
significant iteration
My
dialectical translation
This
bellowed declaration
Of my own independence.

clockwork

hearts are flesh pocket clocks
grandfather clauses
ceaselessly beating me senseless
with their
probable and hollow causes
there is no intent here
only the tick tocking
of established knocking
on poor living doors,
attempted unlocking,
breaking in,
and walking back out.
mutation is a petty way to tip the scales
predictable,
permissible,
no care for details,
my heart reminds
my makeshift mind
as i beat in time
like clockwork.

The Other Colors

You might think a
Gilded globe will only rise
If you wake up and see it
Through two squinting eyes
And Luna sleeps and she dreams
of her lover, it seems
While machines breathe, watch from afar
See and assume these things
It's bizarre.
How audacious to presume
that the sun and the moon
were ever in tune or opposite

Predictable inconsistencies lie
in huge ape minds
Starving for dichotomies
Ravishing every pure thing
that was or were
or is to be
With comparison or symmetry

It's chaotic
Can't you see?
Don't expect equality
My misery hinders me
As does a lethal dose of glee
But nothing is orderly
Or meant to be
Be honest

Broken or fixed?
What if I'm mixed?
My silverware
has no partner in gold
And it's getting old
Only knowing
Meekness or boldness

My first kiss
was nervous
but nothing about firstness
has meaning or purpose
We're feigning awareness
but I couldn't care less
about my first kiss.

And no I don't eat schisms.
Cheap white meat
is a meager feast
Cooked thoroughly
Until it's burnt black.

I crave a
Spectral treat
as it was or were
or is to be
Let me see
the other colors
I want to see
the other colors.

Exoskeleton Necklace

I refuse to fill up my shell with
Limpet flesh
And no one wants the stinking remains of a mussel,
its brains or its body,
Swollen and salty,
Rotting in the sun.
No one decorates a home
with a mass of abalone innards
Some suck it for dinner,
But the winner scrapes the flesh and takes the shell,
And he's a sinner who tastes it as well.
I'm not meant to be eaten
Meat sweetened with spices
In spite of my vices
I'm tender and raw–
But I won't fill my maw
with mollusk flesh
And I won't be caught in some fisherman's mesh
Unless to be made into jewelry
And strung around my own neck.

Clementine

clementine–
now you're no longer mine
you belong to the earth
and i know that that's worth
more than penny or dime
but clementine
was it really your time?
your clock had to stop
before it began to unwind
it's uncanny the way
i imagined you'd find
your place on this earth
but now you're inside
and clementine
my heart doesn't know
what to miss
why to cry
who to kiss
goodnight
who's clear blue eyes
would find their way to mine
because clementine
your life was one that so briefly shined
but your sweet heart beat
is stuck in my mind–
my dear, you are
the reoccurring kind.

Plastic Plants

Plastic plants grow when you're not looking
Virgins to soil
Wire stems uncoil
Purple petals unfurl and settle
In static display like a sample photograph in a hallway
The frame might as well be empty.
Plastic plants grow when you're not looking
Material grapevines might under faint white lamp light
Struggling to feel brightness
It's a fruitless fight
A bitter wine produced when pressed.
But in the presence of less, plastic grapes don't shrivel- they harden.
Fostering false gardens is no mess
No need to get your hands dirty.
Plastic plants grow when you're not looking, so look away–
Allow paper roots to falter
Fabric flowers fray
An array of fresh daisies is outside the foyer
Pushing themselves up to get a better view of true imitation.
(What lies outside rises eye-height
Sucking sunlight righteously,
But plastic plants grow when you're not looking.)

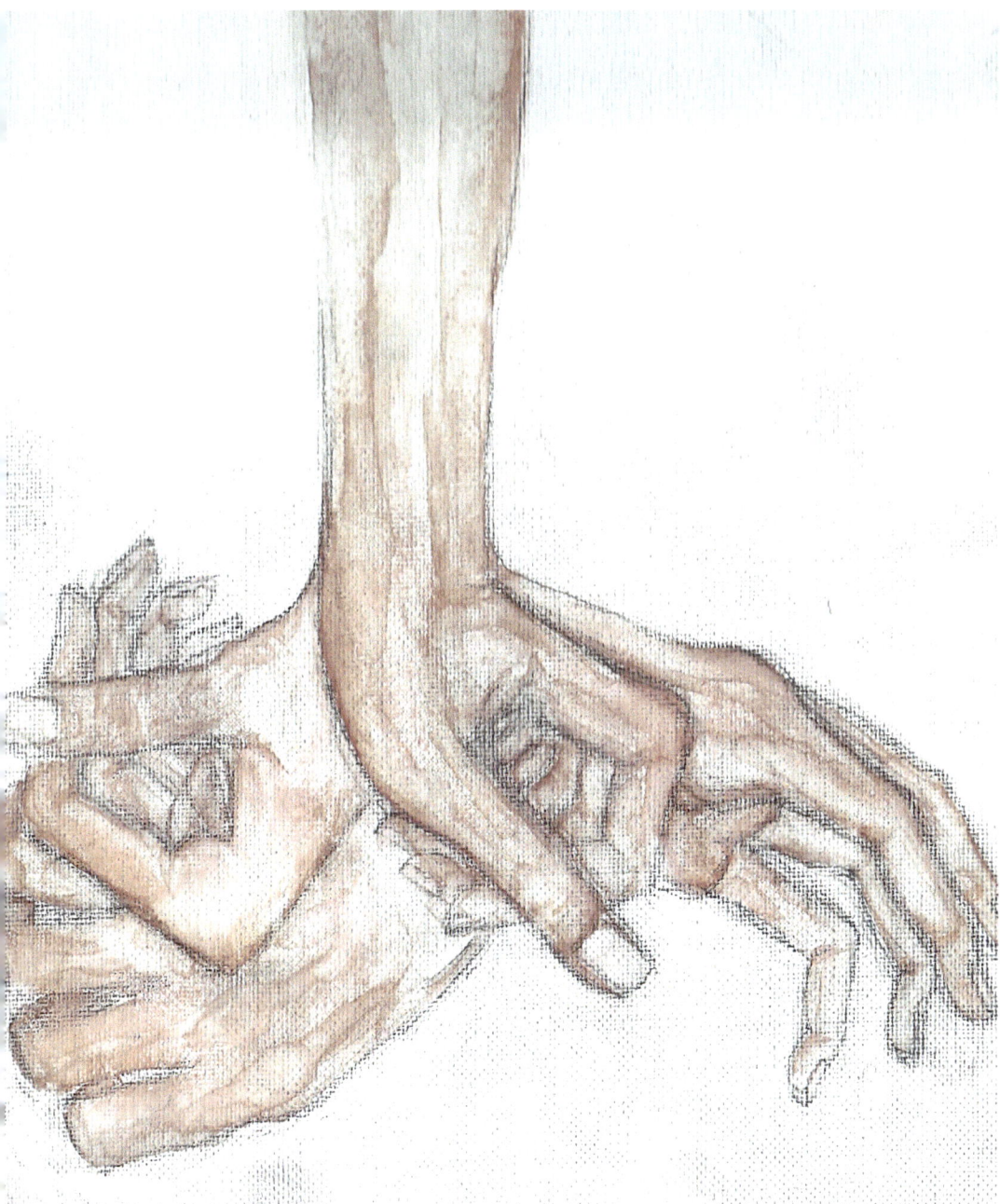

a brief encounter

impermanence traced
her fingers down my cold cheek
fleeting forgiveness

five lines defrosted
she withdrew her slender hand
and left my face striped

Just Some Smut

Offer me your concept
I want to
Consider your topic
I'd like to
Meticulously pick it apart
Lift and tear it
Arrange and pair it
Lick it and see if it sticks

Uncuff and
Offer me your tricks
You'd
Say that
Sleeveless shirts
Don't have enough mystery
Would it be too bold to hold
that history
Has less to write than
You and I
Here talking unreservedly
So fervidly so
So deservedly so

I want to know
Your idea
And it's okay if you
provoke me–

Talk dirty to me
But only in riddles

You may
Tiptoe through my forest mind
Leaving trails of crumbs behind
I'll follow them back to their source.

A lyrical feast
Feed me
I need
A steady supply of
linguistic lies
To keep me on my feet

I refuse to be neat
I will lick your palm and ask for more
Yes I will eat
letters individually
Pop them like cherries
Combining them only for taste
No bread will break
No caloric waste
Your saxophone syntax
Brought close to climax
It's a
Gourmet meal for two

A minimal lunch pack
I'll watch you in IMAX
And paste my interpretation on your forehead
so that maybe
Dessert will be on me

abc song

a shy kiss on a singer's lips
feels a lot like the way
that she might sing an A
and the sting of a bee
(as it seems to me)
is a lot like the bite
of a night out at sea

Women in Linen Sheets

I gave inches of skin to women in linen sheets
I lined their beds with slivers of me
And with a white, lacy frame
They repaid me
With withering grace as a willow who weeps
Or the honeybee's buzzing which lulls them to sleep
Each woman's face is a mirror of mine
Symmetric integrity's quite hard to find
The pulp of the orange or merely the rind
Wholeness is foraged in forests divine.
With palms open and closed
The women disclosed
Tainted images of protruding ribs
Reminiscent of Eden's first limbs
Side by side the heathens lie
And harmonize with honeybee hymns.
Their close eyes see the sunrise beneath the willow tree
Every color is silver, every face is me
Nothing comes cheap in a hospital cot
Wrappings cost every trapping you've got
You're rotting beneath the gauze
It's dead white like a dove
Stained red with love liquid
Dozens of women in clean linen sheets wallow and weep to willow tree
sleep
Lullabies ring in a honey sweet hum
Each tries to sing with lips gone numb
And the sound produced is that of a bee-
The kind that stings and falls at my feet.

Baby

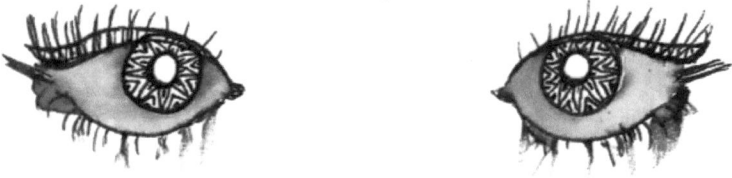

Baby reclines, head heavy.
A pink fleshy face is dimpled
I'd say it's turned into a seat cushion
When baby contorts with need, it's loud.
Cries out no, no and don't want?
Want more? Need more? I am uncomfortable?
Baby language is melodic and piercing—
Unripe squeaky clean tennis shoes split ears when they kick.
The baby kicks and swallows spit and shrieks.
A body bobbles while a soft head draws
exclamation marks on a soft quilt
Baby's head is too heavy to lift
Baby reclines.

Confession on a Spring Day

The woman next door scrubs her porous skin
Soaks sin in a baptismal bathtub
How many clear liters have permeated this membrane?
She swells.
Quarantine warrants explanation, but her mouth is full
And the woman next door,
Who swore she'd speak, somewhere in a survey
Sits silent and peeks through the window.

Imagine her in orange light
Thriving on the dry concrete outside
Ringing out in the heat,
A sweet plea, a sparkling testimony on her upper lip
Just as easily secreted as drawn up by the sun-
Is heard and is Risen.
I imagine she contracts and ripens this
Dehydration like a new awakening,
The grey is stained black with drink
With un-drink
And the woman next door is pardoned as she had been
By the man-made road and the states of matter and the stars.

The woman next door absorbs guilt in
Her damp apartment and becomes holy by cleanly association
Soaking in her mistakes like a cell.

She is also in orange light
Thriving on the dry concrete outside
Letting herself sweat.

Sanctify the fumbled line the gravelly battle cry.
Emergent pleading,
innately impeding,
it's
enjambed with more body than spirit
pulsing and bleeding out.
Hallow now the shadow space, paced in time
and
braced for the fall.
Damned divine,
I might not call it mine and yet it takes my call.

Apple Red- A notice

Today, I'm nostalgic for the present.
Presence is fragile:
Touch with clean fingers
Unclench your fists
Tragedy lingers on laundry lists
You wrote when you were angry.
Milk and bread and
Hurt and Red
Of these
Fruitless figments, these pigments that fade
The most potent defense allows for a trade:
A submission to nightfall in favor of day
Today
I am what I make last
Not that which invades
A sullen seasick kind of mindset
Some haven't quite found other kinds yet
But I think it's time to
Redefine to
Appraise relations
Until it's so that
I accept every blow
Every wink and slow dance
"Get in the car"s
Boredom and entrancement
Following stars
My four year old advancement
Learning my 'r's
Until I approve of my loudest cries
My dripping morals and bloodshot eyes
And the moment I was so tired and high
That my bed melted around me and I felt notably cozy
The moment I was so awake that I reconsidered the severity of my
caffeine addiction and thought about giving it up for a few seconds
before getting distracted or something.

That time when I was so tired that I couldn't lift my limbs anymore and lost confidence in the notion that giving up is a choice–
The moment I was so awake that I, having stayed up all night, wrote this poem at sunrise.
We can be proud of our every action
And I say our because our collective traction
Just might begin to get a grip on it.
We are all in it,
In a forgiving and fervent search
For righteousness
In any sense
A confident consciousness
Collecting twigs of priceless actions-
Stringing them together to be reenacted-
A pretty nest of memories
For future tense treasuries
You can make this nest a home
Unmeasurable entities
Assembled
To resemble
An apple
Red.
The color of care
Not just love-
It's bloodshed
It's warfare
If passion were rationed
I'd be a cheat
Take your fair share
One for you, one for me?
Bullshit.
I'll eat red apples off the ground
Digesting existence in real time, surround sound-
This instance is a privilege
And it can be riveting
if you want it to be,
If you care.

All that's real's
Within and without you,
Surrounding and inside of you
Right here right now.

Notice:
A given moment
analyzed in high detail
yields trees of resonances;
And even though in viewing laterally,
each consequent branch is increasingly pixelated,
And when an apple falls,
each further echo grows increasingly quieter,
Even though the sweet taste will eventually cease to linger,
Red transcends specific site,
The concept of the taste
lives on in the rites of
Those who care, and those who might.
On the tips of the tongues of the ones who tried,
And marinating in the minds
of those who tasted the fruit.

Notice:
In a moment
There is value to the last drop.
And I intend to spend this space and time
Until my body stops.

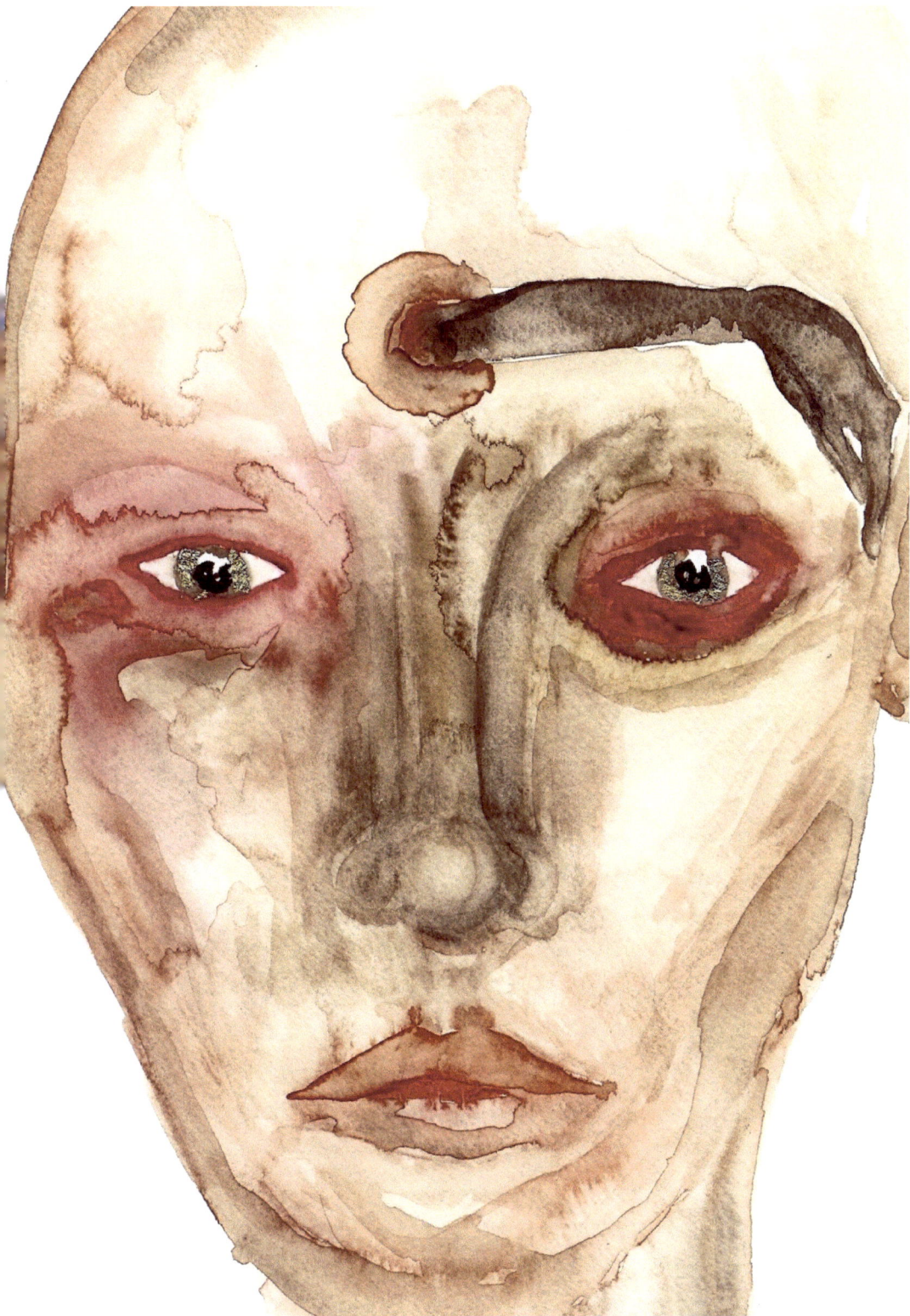

www.ingramcontent.com/pod-product-compliance
Lightning Source LLC
Chambersburg PA
CBHW041530090426
42738CB00035B/27